Praise for
HISTORY AND OTHER POEMS

Memory, culture, and language are the compelling cornerstones of *History and Other Poems*. In this magnificent evocative of the long ago past, Brenda Marie Osbey brings her amazingly accurate voice and probing vision to bear on an historical archive of the Americas from fifteenth through the nineteenth centuries and expresses her powerful twenty-first century reflections on the origins and imposition of the Atlantic slave trade. Exploits and exploitations mingle in the voyages of European explorers, merchants, and slavers and in the words of lost captives, dreamers, and workers in sugar, rice, indigo, or cotton. No pandering to stereotypes and no longing for idealizations here; Osbey reaches deep into her own brilliant imagination and into cultural memory to expose to new life a necessary but often buried history.

— Thadious M. Davis, author of *Southscapes: Geographies of Race, Region, and Literature*

Brenda Marie Osbey is not just a poet *from* New Orleans; rather, she is the poet *of* New Orleans. Osbey is a native New Orleanian, and her work has been colored from the start by Louisiana's extraordinarily mixed, Creole culture. Congo rhythms, the disciplined improvisations of Provençal troubadour and jazz musician blend in the vernacular heartbeat of her best poems. As an African American poet, Osbey is painfully conscious of the mixture of French, British, and Spanish exploration and exploitation that underpins both Louisiana's "créolité" and the global construction of race. In fierce, visceral, mesmeric, incantatory lines, Osbey's *History and Other Poems* demands to know "the real measure of human loss" caused by those twin constructions. Confronting the baleful legacy — all too readily disavowed — of the trade in human beings on which our modern world is founded, these riveting poems plunge the reader so physically into Atlantic history one can taste the blood and sweat and mucus, hear the beat of heart and drum and tide, feel the yielding flesh and hard but brittle bone. Not since Aimé Césaire have we had such a global or such a visceral take on the bloody chains that have yoked Europe, Africa, the Caribbean, and the Americas together. Not since Nina Simone have we heard such brilliant artistry in transforming anger into music.

— Simon Lewis, Associate Director of the Carolina Lowcountry and Atlantic World Program

Anointed with complexities, *History and Other Poems* is superbly executed. Brenda Marie Osbey's poems invite exploration of the chaos and créolité of history. They urge us to attend to their nuances, to be renewed by radical, rich aesthetic permutations. In her previous collections — *Ceremony for Minneconjoux, In These Houses, All Saints: New and Selected Poems*, and *Desperate Circumstance, Dangerous Woman* — Osbey acknowledged her sustained research and investments in history. *History and Other Poems* confirms her poetic mastery of time, space, and narrative, her authority to guide us in the process of becoming enlightened by the profound structures of existence. This is a rare book that secures our participation in and control of the dialogic imagination.

   — Jerry W. Ward, Jr., author of *The Katrina Papers: A Journal of Trauma and Recovery* and Famous Overseas Professor, Central China Normal University (Wuhan)

Place this new book by Brenda Marie Osbey next to the work of Eduardo Galeano. After centuries, after Columbus, after the long era of discovery, comes the daughter of a new Negritude. Brenda Marie Osbey is a language explorer, a navigator of metaphors and stories. She understands that what cannot be erased becomes memory. Yes, there is "no history of this world that is not written in black." When civilizations clash poets are born. How long have we been waiting for Brenda Marie Osbey?

   — E. Ethelbert Miller, Director of the African American Resource Center, Howard University

Interviewed for the *Faubourg Tremé* documentary amidst Hurricane Katrina's devastation, a visibly shaken Brenda Marie Osbey didn't bow down. Her courage made a never-to-be-forgotten impression on the film's countless viewers. In *History and Other Poems*, she has forged her grief, her anger, and her passion into an equally unforgettable tribute to her ancestral city. It is a matchless gift to Osbey's admirers both at home and abroad. And for those who want to know what New Orleans means, it is required reading.

In her "little history part one," Osbey disses the "wearied and wearying lessons" of an invented past. Her subjects inhabit a world of European conquest, deadly microbes, filthy slave fort dungeons, horrific ocean crossings, and chattel slavery on sugar plantations from the Caribbean to Louisiana. In the arc of Osbey's lessons, there "is no history of this world that is not written in black."

In conjuring the "nearness of our slave-i-tude," she cuts to the heart of slavery's lived reality and its 21st-century legacy. Like her New Orleans literary forebears, she understands the city's genius and the necessity of getting its history right. She does exactly that in this brilliant *tour de force*.

   — Caryn Cossé Bell, author of *Revolution, Romanticism, and the Afro-Creole Protest Tradition in Louisiana, 1718-1868*

Brenda Marie Osbey's new poetic sequence deepens the historical record of the Atlantic world with poetic truth; her probing metaphors are never less than figures of thought representing the archetypal drama of the period that still shapes the power relations of our own.

"History" is a major production . . . remarkably successful in providing us with what academic scholarship typically neglects or finds so hard to capture, namely felt history. . . . Osbey's poem is a brilliant exercise in cultural archaeology — reminiscent of Robert Hayden's groundbreaking poem "Middle Passage." No detail . . . is without significance.
 — William Boelhower, literary editor of *Atlantic Studies* and editor of *New Orleans in the Atlantic World*

Brenda Marie Osbey has weaved history into the rich texture of an epic poetry that only she can write: the fascinating, disquieting voices and sounds of sensuality, rage, power, beauty, death, voices speaking intimately through the censored chapters of history, now brought back to life.
 — Rédouane Abouddahab, Professor of American Studies, Université Louis Lumière – Lyon II, France

Nothing better describes the work of Brenda Marie Osbey than the phrase "truth and beauty," although I might, on second thought, prefix this with "powerful." You cannot help but wonder how deep is the well she reached into to bring us such language.
 — Charles E. Cobb, Jr., Chair of the Middle Passage Ceremonies and Port Markers Project Advisory Board, and Visiting Professor in the Department of Africana Studies at Brown University

The beauty of Osbey's poetry lies in its depth, in its ability to call up multiple realities, to expose the layers of social, cultural, familial, and individual history. . . . In her poetry, memory creates a spectral space in which the dead and living coexist and change one another.
 — Shari M. Evans, University of Massachusetts – Dartmouth. "Spectral Space: Memory, Loss, and Reclamation in the Poetry of Brenda Marie Osbey"

But Osbey's poems walk the line of danger. They recall dangerous people; they wield dangerous words. Her work will speak to you of the familiar in ways that make it strange; it will speak to you of the unfamiliar in terms that you know you've heard before.
 — Evie Shockley, Writers at Rutgers Reading Series, Rutgers University

In *History and Other Poems*, Brenda Marie Osbey brilliantly puts her hand inside our history, toting the heft of centuries, and pulls out wisdom that is newer than the latest scheme of human domination. Not since Robert Hayden's "Middle Passage" has the rape of Africa been so devastatingly told.
— Joanne V. Gabbin, Executive Director, Furious Flower Poetry Center, James Madison University

"History is your own heartbeat." So wrote Michael Harper. Few poets have attended to America's beating, bleeding heart as closely and as tenderly as Brenda Marie Osbey. In these poems, as in her past work, she traces the mortal marks our past has left on our city streets, in the rhythms of our feet. If history has been a coffle, it is also our freedom train.
— Aldon Nielsen, author, *Black Chant: Languages of African American Postmodernism* and *Mantic Semantic*, Kelley Professor of American Literature, Pennsylvania State University

After the myths, the fables, the abridgments, the approximations, and the outright lies that masquerade in its name, what, then, is history? Osbey asks then answers this most prosaic of questions, in the most magical form. Traversing centuries, circling the globe, by land and sea, these bewitching poems bear the stamp of her linguistic dexterity, her vernacular range, her Olympian intellect, her sheer poetic heft and genius. With this volume, Osbey establishes once more — just as she has in volumes past — that her name will be/is indeed already writ large in the history of the narrative poem, in the world's pantheon of treasures.
— Deborah McDowell, Alice Griffin Professor of English at the University of Virginia

HISTORY

AND

OTHER POEMS

BOOKS BY BRENDA MARIE OSBEY

Ceremony for Minneconjoux   (1983)
In These Houses   (1988)
Desperate Circumstance, Dangerous Woman   (1991)
All Saints: New and Selected Poems   (1997)
History and Other Poems   (2012)

HISTORY
AND
OTHER POEMS

BY
BRENDA MARIE OSBEY

Time Being BookS

An imprint of Time Being Press
St. Louis, Missouri

Time Being Books®
10411 Clayton Road
St. Louis, Missouri 63131

Time Being Books® is an imprint of Time Being Press®, St. Louis, Missouri.

Time Being Press® is a 501(c)(3) not-for-profit corporation.

Time Being Books® volumes are printed on acid-free paper.

ISBN 978-1-56809-179-2 (paperback)

Library of Congress Cataloging-in-Publication Data:

Osbey, Brenda Marie.
  History and other poems / by Brenda Marie Osbey. — 1st ed.
     p. cm.
  ISBN: 978-1-56809-179-2 (pbk. : alk. paper)
  I. Title.
  PS3565.S33H57 2012
  811'.54—dc23

                                                    2012040022

Cover design by Jeff Hirsch
Cover and frontispiece: detail of Martin Waldseemüller's 1507 world map
Book design and typesetting by Trilogy M. Mattson

Manufactured in the United States of America
First Edition, first printing (2012)

ACKNOWLEDGMENTS

This collection evolved over a number of years, following the drafting and development of the title poem. Along the way, both it and I have benefited enormously from the sustained support of organizations, institutions and individuals. The Camargo Foundation at Cassis, France, supported the first phase of research and writing during my 2004 tenure as writer-in-residence there. The Carolina Lowcountry and Atlantic World (CLAW) Program at the College of Charleston featured the first public reading of the poem as part of its 2008 "Ending the International Slave Trade: a Bicentenary Inquiry" conference. And, in 2010, a somewhat different version of the poem was published in the United Kingdom-based journal *Atlantic Studies: Literary, Historical and Cultural Perspectives*.

Earlier versions of other poems in this collection were published in the following periodicals: "Qu'on arrive enfin (une histoire en cours/a tale in-progress)," the original French/English version in *Renaissance Noire*, 2004 and *MondesFrancophones.com: Revue Mondiale des Francophonies*, 2009; "Canne à Sucre: a Slave-Song Suite" in *The American Poetry Review*, 2005; and the original French/English version of "L'Abécédaire DOM-TOM/DOM-TOM Primer" in *Illuminations: An International Magazine of Contemporary Writing*, 2007, and the French in *MondesFrancophones. com: Revue Mondiale des Francophonies*, 2009.

The author gratefully acknowledges the assistance and support also of the American Studies Association (ASA); Association Française d'Études Américaines (AFEA); the Carter G. Woodson Institute for African American and African Studies of the University of Virginia; Centre d'Analyse et de Recherche du Monde Anglophone (CARMA); the Dillard University African World Studies Department; the Embassy of the United States in Paris and its consular offices at Toulouse, Marseille and Lyon; Université Louis Lumière – Lyon II; Université Paul Valéry – Montpellier III; and especially, the Africana Studies Department of Brown University.

Grateful aknowledgement is made also to Paul Allen, Houston A. Baker, Jr. and Charlotte Pierce Baker, Alain Beullard, Dave Brinks & the 17 Poets! Weekly Reading Series, Judy Ebner & Paul Vernon, Dorothea Fischer-Hornung, Trudier Harris, Henry C. Lacey, Alexandre Leupin, John Wharton Lowe, Norman Roussell, Susan Fitch Spillman, and the late Daniel C. Thompson.

Special appreciation is due to my attorney and lifelong friend, Roy J. Rodney, Jr. and always, to my brother, Lawrence C. Osbey, Jr., who first introduced me to mythology, cartography and the applied study of history.

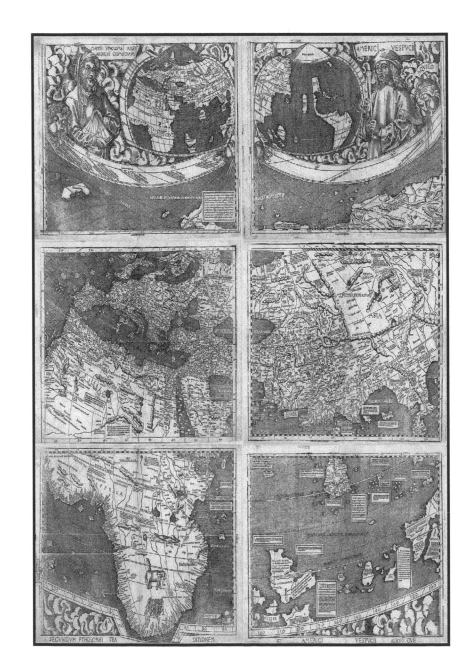

This book is dedicated to J. B. Borders IV —
in love
blood
sugar
brick
iron
breath
the heft of centuries —
more —
even more.

CONTENTS

HISTORY
AND
OTHER POEMS

Qu'on Arrive Enfin (a tale in-progress)

1

and so we arrive at last in our native land —
the earth itself marked by slavery.
up there, in the open air, the stink, the hot funk of hot blood
the rowdy rebel-niggers of the past.
funny, no?
how we always return to this —
the city, the life
that slavery built,
tales altogether invented
as told by historians, founding fathers, the church.
but we are sick and tired of lies, dirty tricks and fraud,
we are sick of tales and of historians
sick of indigo, tobacco, rice and rum
we are sick of king-cotton and sugar cane
sick of it all
and can only wish hard-hard-hard
that the lakes, the bayous, swamps large and small
will have swallowed it all
flooded
erased it all.

but then
we don't bother about this, really
because there's always (the chance of) hurricane.

therefore, down with the dealers in blood and in flesh

long live the conquering hurricane
long live the leveling swamp
long live the rowdy rebel-niggers and the bad little niggers as well.
let there remain not one single plantation to reek of the stench of roasted
flesh-and-blood.

2

and so i ask myself,
what would suffice?
and my answer,
nothing. not a single thing.
as long as ever i live nothing nothing nothing shall ever suffice it.

3

used to be
a good while back
used to be
they'd chop heads over far less.

and how many bloody heads *would* have rolled back then?

     and so every time we hear the word "creole" —
          or better still "le monde créole" —

     the fetid breath of the slavers and their lesser merchantmen

     and the great stench of their women taking their little whores'-baths
               only every three days or so

and so what?
what's it to us we ask ourselves from time to time
a thousand times over
what's it to us?

used to be
used to be
once
upon
a time

4

and i can not   quite fathom   it

all.

5

what then is history?
hardly even fable
hardly even myth —
nothing but the lies repeated by masters and their henchmen
nothing but lines repeated ad nauseam
in order to memorize them well enough
in order to entertain themselves well enough
until time for slashing the throat of one of their negresses
      only after having fucked her good and raw

oh it's the factories
the accounting-houses
over there
just along the river
where they produce
neither grain nor sugar nor anything else —
the "social science" of slavery

Répétez s'il-vous-plait
Répétez s'il-vous-plait
      Tous à la fois à la fois à la fois . . .

Slaves to the City

we stand in line to receive our daily bread.
it has the taste of sand
like so much else in this country
where there is no sand.
we move along the red-bricked streets
all of one piece.
we stop from time to time
to stare at buildings.
we do not know
have never seen such riches
and such places — and so many —
for the storing up of riches.
we are numb.
we move about together — all of one piece.
we stand.
we stare.
we eat our bread of sand and then move on.

where are the young
the children
the very old
our holy men and women
and our saints?
where are our sacred objects?
the little gods to carry on our persons
now that the great god sleeps?
we do not ask these questions of one another.
we do not dare.
we know our own small piece of truth each one of us.
nor do we share such truths.

we look into one another's eyes and faces
read nation, gods, wars.
we ask ourselves who will betray us today and whom we shall
betray and
for what cause?
we do not ask the things we need to know —

we do not dare.

we eat the bread of sand.
we move along the red-bricked streets
stare into faces —

nations, gods, and wars.

Canne à Sucre: a Slave-Song Suite

your lips against me in the dark
expanse of face and shoulders
feel of back and breastbone
nothing but what they
are
how when you look
then history makes sense
comfort consolation
the many uses of the body
words such as flesh meat undulation unguent funk
desire claim urgent flesh consume motion flesh

to live in desire
to live one's own desire —
and neither consolation nor despair —
to smell and taste how we cleave together and apart
my hand inside your middle
history there —
fruit left on a sill deep into summer —
my grandmother's clean cool and perfect hands on my cheeks
and i held between her knees looking up
brown hands folded across her skirted lap
her own so cool and perfect hands —
roof-tile slate grey eyes
full of memory and of longing —
i long for you now —
your face across generations
desire

akin to gluttony
bitter brown of cane
and warm inside
as the moment rum
explodes its silence in the waiting mouth
— a wish? —
aguardiente the slave-men say
aguardiente
agua como amor
su amor como agua, mi señor, slave-women respond —
in full view
brick walls old as cities old in time
brick walls older than the many deaths breathed into them so —
agua y tierra, mi señor
agua y tierra y sangre, papí
agua ardiente como amor —
i see you through my grandmother's eyes
roof-slate grey
i feel her hands in yours
the love she bore down into ash:
he consoled me, she said for no reason one day
consoled me.
and the twins were born.

often in the middle of an afternoon
a train calls
hooting its way to present tense

your dark hand on my thigh
consoling
driving
invoking
a kind of collapse we come to long for once we've known
comes unasked
resisted ill-defined
shuddering from somewhere underneath
the bowels
and fear of biblical proportion
and then we bear
into

the heft of centuries
blood and sugar borne living from some field outside the city
sugar that burns
into teeth and lips and gums
consolation
the nearness of our slave-i-tude —
inside the city
free-women in tignons and turbans
leaf sandals wrapping their feet
copper and gold ringing ankles and wrists
brown and naked beneath single-layered dresses
"made for loving" the old ones cluck and watch them go
"born for it" the only known response —
sting of sugar and of blood lacing the milk they pass into the warm
                                                        mouths of
their own infants
their men —
and fingers and lips that circle and smile
and the dreaming that does not shy away
but sucks and sucks until the cane is soft
soft as bagasse —
"you sweetness you" the old say to the young
ma canne à sucr'

i turn to you in bed centuries
of made-for-loving hammering in my head and thighs
canne à sucre i mouth into your mouth
bed of moss
brick walls and floors
your hands like coffee
roasted
ready to serve up
sweetness
(ah, ma douceur)
lips of a woman
or small child
eternal kiss from where the cane grows straight tall pliant beyond dreams

back breastbone and hands and lips

consume

consume

consume away

the burning building up the dying again
born to it
borne
as warriors are born —

brown babies carrying history like sacks of yam to market —
born to consume away
to die resurrect
claim motion urgent meat desire
claim undulation claim consume
claim flesh
to cleave
and cleave
together and apart
and warm inside —
how when you look they are nothing but what you
live

in
against in all

the dark
and bitter brown of
cane.

DOM-TOM Primer

les DOM
les TOM
le beau patrimoine

les dom
yé les tom

there is a certain kind of woman
who offers herself like an eden
and so one does whatever one wants with her
one does whatever one can with her
so long as one pays the bills
or at least signs the receipts.

there is a certain kind of land one walks on
without the least sense
of even being in this world down here.
they usually produce
bananas
pineapples
wonderful spices
all sorts of foods
sweet and peppery —
exotique —
they have names like —
well, they don't really have names so we have to name them.
and once they're named

we write them on maps of the conquered world
the vanquished world
and because we're humanitarians
we begin civilizing them.
and because we're interested in their good
we have to humanize them.
and to really humanize them
we have to study them,
anthropologize them
and to really study them —
and because we're such humanitarians —
we have to fuck them.
yes, to really humanize them
a good fucking is what's needed.
and all the while we're fucking them
we're also giving them lessons in civilization.
because we're humanitarians after all.
and that's good.
oui c'est bon
it's good to have that sense

of fucking
a whole people
a whole world —
oui —
to have the sense
of never enough
but then we've got to finish
got to conquer, vanquish, master
conquer and vanquish and master
because if not
if not
we'll have to sign the damned receipts.
we'll have to
because we're very humanitarian after all.
but one of these days
some woman's going to come carrying iou's.
and that's how we make
the *DOM*
the *TOM*
because it was *si bon*
that almost-ancient fuck-session
the DOM
the TOM
the heritage
ya-bòn

ya-bòn
comme ça
et ça
so that it's never finished.

O — the DOM
the TOM
comme ça
patri-
moine.

2

and what if one of these days
what if one of these days we were to finish with all this
                                        dom-tom-foolerie?
what if we decided to give up the taste for bananas and
                                        pineapples?
but what for?
all the best colonies are already taken back.
all we can do now
is *eat* the fruit of our labors.
it's not exactly easy civilizing the whole world like that —
or almost the whole world —
britain —
though no longer "great" —
played her part as well.
oui.
for back then, the world was so much bigger than today.
now there's nothing left.
it's over.
the world today — ruined —

nothing but minor countries, all pouting.
they're all finished, all of them.
and we
we eat some few pitiful bananas
and dream of lost years.
and so we have to eat them.
gulp them down.
swallow them whole if need be.
absolutely.
and if it were up to me to decide
i'd pass some new laws
so that the french
would eat bananas
every
damned day.
comme ça.

Regarding the Intermediate Travels of Cristóval Colón

Book the Second of the Admiral

i loved my father and my father loved me.
but it was never my dream to be a weaver.
i saw the bright ships sail
nor
do i know the first time i heard the word *spices*
but in that word
was magic
and gold
and more than gold
more than adventure
for there lay fame
bright and simple
as a clear day for sailing.
it was never my aim to be only a sailor.
nor was there nothing for me
in the turning out of cloths.

san salvador
marie galante
cap haitien —
such lands.
my own italy
even sea-going portugal
what did they know of such dreams?
mine was a soul already inclined
to greatness.

and when i went into the church there at la rábida
and looked upon the emblems blazoned there
i knew i had come upon my rights
and that good and catholic soldier isabel
could give more
than all the known desirings of
this heart.
and so i went to work.

my father was a simple man, a weaver.
he never could know the pull and heave of my heartstrings for the sea.

spices.
that was all my dream.
spices and the sea
and my name writ large in the great and handsome book of history.
will they recall, do you believe, how i all but alone, all alone really,
invented the *notion* of admiralty?

o seville city of a merchant's dreams
city that was my undoing
city that never was
and i shall have my own city said i to my brothers as a boy.
laugh if you will
but i shall have my very own city
streets paved in gold and every spice and peppered thing
and i will share with you if only you help me to find my way
out on the sea.
yes the sea is the only way to achieve the unknown lands.
laugh if you will.
laugh if you must.
but help me get my way upon that sea.

and so began my life as a navigator.
a boy of fourteen i was
and ripe with it.
already a mariner at trade before i was a man.

and if the sea cannot make a man of you then nothing will.
for she is a hard mistress
and brooks no infidelity —

o santa santa fé
was all my prayer in those days —
i cannot tell the hardships that she taught me.
i would not tell you if i could.

and then i read old ptolemy's cosmography
and learned to gaze the stars.
then i was sick with it as i never was sick before.
then planetary bodies made me hunger
just as the sea had made me thirst.
and i was mad for it
mad
and right they were to say it
but not in that manner.
what *can* they know of such dreams such hope?
land and sea
and land and sea
and everywhere savage hordes
half-naked gleaming
gleaming sweating reeking of humanity
and i lord admiral of those seas and more
who gave themselves to me
and gifts and foods besides.
who among you would not round the whole wide globe to be a king
where never man had ever yet set foot?
and pagans looked upon you as a god come from the sea?
and concubines of every heathen sort
swoon into death after bedding only some few times?
or else bearing onto the earth legs spread apart without a note of shame
and from the bloody mess of their loins a bastard son or daughter
heaved upon those dying breasts for some last glimpse?
worlds i tell you

worlds vaster than this strip you call the civilizing world.
such things i have seen with my own eyes.
such babes i have dandled and cooed.
who are you to judge me in the end?
who have never stepped beyond your fair genoa or minor tongue-tied lisboa?
who all will die some day of old age on a hard chair for your throne?
in spain they call me cristóbal the great.
my seed is scattered over islands you will never see.
> there was a maiden
> and yes i venture to call her so although
> she was a true confirmèd heathen and right proud
> her name some bright vexation of syllables she tried to teach
> > me laughing
>
> but i had other uses for my time and hers and named her isola.
> isola
> daughter of that pagan prince —
> *o isola of my broken seed*
> and i will die never knowing the brood you carried in your loins
> > for me
>
> and only lady dona felipa for my compensation.

for such is youth:
marry well and bring forth catholic sons.

when king affonso wrote to me
he did counsel me thus.
and i obeyed.
and i obeyed.
and not one piece of portugal's gold ever crossed my out-turned hand.

yes such is youth.

around and around the world
and still i am longing for my city
genoese in my heart that i am
and woven of thick hardy stuffs
i carry on
as
even now
bright ships
bright ships
i close my eyes
and still the bright ships beckon the while
to farther and to ever farther seas.

isabel and her father confessor and their king —
it was they who made me admiral
sovereign of all the seas
after the goddamned moors had cost me years of revenues.

17000 ducats.
a great sum to me then.
and came a time i tossed as much in trinkets
for the favors of a good and catholic king.
colonies
whole peoples have been named for my discoveries.
genoese you call me still?
no gentlemen.
you do not know me.
you do not know me and shall not judge me
ever.

around the world
around
the world
and no i never did find my fabled city.
she would be
cast in gold and in copper
she would be redolent in ointments and in spices —
dark savage womb of the world my sea —
and i would name her isola
and gladly die within her walls

an old man i am and do not expect to see more in this life.
i am an old man.
at night i lie upon my chair discomfited and watch the heavens.
some nights they do not come to let me watch them.
and then i dream a young man's dreams —
for i would name her isola.
yes and i would name her isola.

Book the First of the Guanahani

the land we called yamaye
gave riches in metals and produce and spices and more besides.
and they had only to subdue
my father, prince of the caribs
a seafaring people of great will and character and beauty.

they say that when my sister saw the stranger
she begged our father to give him to her as a gift.
and being a prince of good wisdom he would not.
but my sister was spoiled and feted and the daughter of the prince.
what was to be done with her?
and so he gave the savage to her for a plaything.

and now here am i — guardian of the waste he strewed among us.
descended from the gods from the part of our mother
she chose to soil us
all of us with the stink of that old foreigner.
and she gave to her daughters bright foolish names —
marie galante, dominica, navidad, juana, española —
gibberish he cried out in drunken rages,
and she drunk with him
lurching from tobacco and aguardiente.
i see her even now
my mother's daughter
no better than the whores they tell of in those lands
the two who ever did return alive —
ironical that she
should live to see them spread out dead before her — daughters every one —
and she persisting alone and in pain unto the end
the foul-smelling sores he gave her oozing down her legs.
at least she let him name her isola
so that perhaps we will one day forget how wide
the daughter of the prince
did spread her legs
to populate these islands
in the highest hours of the sun
while the gods were drowsing.
who would believe that
same disease that turned her womanhood to carrion
would also take away her sense?
"my daughters will be tutored at the court of the queen of expaña!"
she was heard to rave some nights.
i heard her myself

and did not move to help her.
let her stew in it i heard myself curse her.
and felt no shame.
and went instead to comfort our father
who was taking a long time to die in those days
of the sickness in his
soul.

The Book of the Last of the Guanahani

the arawaqi were our younger cousins by marriage between the gods.
and had i not been so desirous to put them in their place
i might have seen what the yxpañaro was plotting at my kingdom
but i was distracted by their impudence
as well as by the complaint of my elder daughter
who would go on until she had her way.
and now she is all but perished from it.
and i have seen in my visions
how i too am dying
slower than a
man of my stature
ever was meant to fall.
as the arawaqi say
the gods are making great feasting on my livers and my heart.
and i have come to the end of days
and now must ask my younger daughter
to set me free.
every day i search her eyes for it.

and every day she shields herself from my sight.
is it love that binds her from the quest?
or hating desire for vengeance?
for foolish as was guantanamexe
as serious is guanaguahana.

surely no man of my stature ever was
meant to be brought low before those others
whose fathers served my fathers
in the oldest house of the gods
before there was time
or the history the yxpañaro wept so for.
my soul is too great
to fall so low.

Codicil of the Warrior Queen

the day i cut the heart out of my father and ate it live
was the day i became the warrior of my own soul.
and when i held my sister's portion out and she refused it raving
there was not a moment's pause until i put the machete to her
and threw the rotting shell of her from the mound.
they call us flesh-eaters?
i will show them the better.
for i have consumed the breaking heart and gizzards of my old father.
they were pierced with fibers of repentance and remorse.
it has made me valiant.
and it has made me pure.

now i am sitting squatting waiting the stranger's return.
now is the time of sacrifice and of destiny.
now i wait to see
another ship of strangers
carrying other evils from other lands.

i squat in the shadows of my green kingdom
guanaguahana
last daughter
of the last lord
of the guanahani
of the race of the gods.
and around and around
this old old world
the bright ships sail
the bright ships sail
bright ships
sail.

History

But I am tired today
of history, its patina'd clichés
of endless evil.
— from "The Islands," by Robert Hayden

and so we begin again our weary wearied and wearying lessons
because we have not learned them well enough.
only this time
without chanties about some ocean-blue
because for us
all oceans are forever red.
and we begin this time without the head and finger count
for what's the real measure of human loss
once figures climb into the tens of tens of thousands
multiplied by however many ships debarking
                                        from however many nations
to archipelagos of death, to continents of doom?
and still for all that chatter
gorée persisting into the red and golden sun
its few hundred or so inhabitants
making the daily ferry run
barely even eye-ing the western born
borne on across unroiling waters —
and boys are playing at games
innocent as all of time.
time and even more time is what has dullened us so.
for we are tired of lessons.
and yet it is to lessons we must go.

the looming sea is all about the wide wide world.
and it is wide
oh yes it is
the world is wide and wide and full of evil ides.
and the history of the world if we would tell it
would strike us all down dead upon the spot marked
with
its greenish stain like money in the poker-men's upturned pot.

oh and oh and i am weary with it all.
and here is yet another castle
another monument to look upon.
and docents with their sad or singing eyes —
the sharp accentuated hush that follows as they speak
men fingering chains and such
and women who will not turn their eyes
and children who look about beneath the words that take so long
                                                         to tell —
the history of this world which if we tell it straight
will kill us all before we even taste the smell of even the most rudimentary
                                                                    hate

on with it then.
then once and once and oh so long ago.
we can only tell so much at any telling.
we have lives — such as they are — and other work to do
and can perhaps only stand the telling of this history
in parts one and two.

in bambara and shango
wolof and peul tshihiba twi éwondo
in sara and sérère
in toupouri hausa mandara boulou
in yoruba kinyarwanda and ki-kongo
and all the languages around the hardy cape then
let us tongue and tongue as the aperture of the hardiest of the *old-line*
trumpeters.
and this time
let us try for once to get it right.
and this time let us tongue it deep and well into the night.

and bring me now the bones of diogo cão
and bring the shroud of pope nicky the vth
bring me the cape of old victor schoelcher
bring me the bastards
and let me have my way
and let it last until i've earned at last my full pay.

(the sun
bright disk cast against the sky
that shines without warming ever
wasted gold set against blue skies that are not mine
nor ever will be.)

o são tomé
o são vicente
o cape o cape of all good hope
elmina and cape coast
île de gorée
cabo de delgado
fort osu

all of them *"ages ago / last night / when we were young"*
shame   shame of ghana
thirty-six of forty-two built there as barter
elmina grandest patroness of them all
wings of floors reconstructed into such grandeur:
"the women's quarters have a most unpleasant, most befoul'd odor"
and thus the viewing balconies up above the sweltering human hum.

fort and forteress

but never you mind about that
for there's enough to go around and then —
300 miles of coast
60 known castles
remains of half as many
undisturbed
monuments to green and gold and silver god

cape coast built by hardy swedes 16 & 53
fort osu 16 & 61 by the very captives who would stand and die
there
rotting blood into the
hard packed earth.

lust for gold
lust for blackest black of gold.
all so much whoring in the veins of a continent laid to waste
trading all along the coast
capturing and herding deep inside the hot interior
"oh, there be wealth enough for plenty,
and kingdom come before we bleeds 'em dry."

"decreed: that greater benin will export no more men as chattels; for to
continue in that way
should only weaken the core of our kingdom."
women and children remain free, however,
to be enslaved at any time.

and kingdom come indeed.

see also
senegambia
liberia
kingdom of kongo
sierra leone
gold coast
ivory coast
bight of biafra
bight of benin
southeast of africa from good hope to delgado and all of madagascar

why is it called cape of good hope?

sugar cotton coffee metals tobacco
shipping finance insurance
industry
such cities as amsterdam, liverpool, bristol
stade-en-lande whitehaven la rochelle and boston
rotterdam newport nantes lisbon
such kingdoms as _____ *(fill in the blank)*
and along north africa herself   indian ocean
and so-called middle east
sahara of shifting footprints

why is it called, do *you* believe, cape of *good* hope?

and then   of course   that red red red red sea

worlds   continents of exclusion
la trahison des clercs
the disironic unwillingness
of colonial powers to self-destruct —

mercantable movable property
chattel
res —
tyrannies of words thrown ad lib against the abject body —

there is no history of this world that is not written in black.

> *The peoples of Europe, having exterminated the*
> *peoples of America, have been obliged to enslave*
> *the peoples of Africa and use them to clear all*
> *these lands for cultivation. Sugar would cost*
> *too much if the plant that produces it were not*
> *tended by slaves.*
> — from "Le droit de rendre les nègres esclaves"
> *De l'Esprit des lois* by Montesquieu

seats of exchange
the counting houses
wealth of the new world:
raw materials   commodities produced
caravel
caravel
a word that floats along the tongue.

sugar rice molasses rum indigo spices cotton
continuing raids
forced marches
slaves and ivory
slaves and gold
raw materials back and forth
back and forth
caravel
a word a world that floats upon the tongue.

No commerce in the world produces as many advantages as that
of the slave trade.
— Colbert

sugar molasses indigo rice spices cotton rum
sugar cotton coffee metals tobacco
indigo rum molasses
rice spices cotton

why does the industrial revolution occur simultaneously with the trade in
black flesh?

i hear someone sayin' —
hunh
the chain
the gang — oh-o-oh
. . . sound of the . . .
i'm'a leave that alone now
— from "Chain Gang," by Sam Cooke

nor does it matter what order we tell it.
only that we know it
once and for every all
know it as we know
our own breathing in the night

sugar cotton coffee metals tobacco
sugar cotton coffee metals tobacco
indigo rum molasses
rice spices cotton
wealth of the new world
> *and old king cotton*
> *his heart was so rotten*
> *they laid him out to die*
> *and here he comes again masquerading as "... the fabric of*
> > *our lives"*

"one day / we'll all be free."

there is a kind of churning in the gut that comes with the
                                                    learning of history.
memory of old sea-sicknesses-unto-death?
a taste of bones ground up to make white bread?
ground up to make
refined white sugar?
polished into
pearl-white rice?
aged twelve years
into light smooth rum?
for the world
the wide wide world is fat
greased on bones from deep in the sea
oh but let us not speak yet of seas
let us never speak of seas
let us look instead across horizons to
other sides of these worlds we know
in the texts of our skins

colón and colonie
exercises in linguistic dexterity
west indies
east indies
french indies
dutch indies
and such
companies:

american islands company
royal african company
french senegal company
santo domingo company
guiana company
second louisiana company
new cayenne company
new france
and that much more
company
so very much
company
how long until application of the etiquette
that a great value of being good company
is knowing when to depart?

code noir   code noir   code noir

noted,
record of a crossing
1625:
five portuguese ships
bearing one thousand two hundred eleven african cargo
of which five hundred eighty-three die in transit
sixty-eight more within the first week of arrival at brazil.

"a little coffee to wake me
a bit of tea to comfort
sugar to sweeten
a taste of rum to cure me
a taste of rum all around
all around
all around
o a good swig o' rum all around"

status report:
1730 till 1780
glory days of the trade on american continent;
1746 till 1774 mortality rate aboard slave ships from nantes harbor
as much as thirty-four per cent.
1754 three hundred thousand enslaved in french west indies alone.
in 1780 numbers rise to six hundred seventy-three thousand there.
1786 good king louis orders improved work conditions:
     no "hard labor" sunset to sunrise —
     first mandate also
     of french two-hour lunch break.

a little leisure
a *little* leisure is a very good thing.
very little leisure so much the better.

status update:
1850 official end of the trade to brazil.
three million six hundred thousand imported later that year.

"so that MAN has indeed become
the coin of Africa . . ."

     sing:
     Sugar for my coffee.
     Sugar for my tea.
     Posies at my footsteps.
     Don't you fancy me?

and when you've finished singing

then bring me the tongue of any who use the word *slave* as metaphor for
                                                                    servitude
metaphor for addiction
as metaphor for love
metaphor for any thing
bring me their tongues
to tack up on the walls of those castles —
o fort and forteress —
by the saddest of the old old seas.
but do not let me speak.
bring me their tongues
no do not let *me* speak at all:

my curse is not even ripened yet.
and my mouth already is filled to the teeth with it.

only more such exercises in linguistic dexterity, in flow

the spanish crown proposes
the french crown proposes
the right christian portuguese king proposes
fra bartolomeo considers
fray bartolome de albornoz dissents

legerdemain by word of mouth
jests of tongue and teeth and palate:

emissary of the crown
explorer
sovereign and sovereignty
requerimiento
encomienda
african slave trade
internecine african warfare
development of 17th century *slaving states*
kidnapping, capture, hunting.
indenture, engagement, servitude.
tawny indian and blackamoor african
O call a spade a spade and get it over with —
human beings endowed with souls and requiring moral care and instruction?
devils in league with some master devil host?
call a slave a slave and be done with it

for *we* never are.
and *it* is never done.
series of ages-old adaptations and adjustments
improvisations and re-orderings
known universes
and concepts of kin
and all night gig rehearsals within the haunted texts of our haunted skin.
"you ain't seen nothing yet."

*"I left my hat / ba-doum-**doum** / in Haiti!"*

        i'll just bet you did
        o i'll just bet
        "just a handful of gimme and a mouthload of
                                much-obliged."

i want to know
i want to know
just tell me where to rest my malediction
for i cannot rest
i cannot rest until i smell that smell of blood
i cannot rest until i have again the sense
that i was born with
that something's rotten
every time i don my garments of yellow cotton
or see the slim black fingers of boys who play piano
or taste the first sip of dark dark rum
or sweeten my coffee
or tread the slave-bricked streets of my own city —
the wastes of downtown streets where
children
sell themselves for fast-food meals of ground meat and grease
and everything is everything
and nowhere is there satisfaction to be had
and the whole of history seems designed to render me sad
disconsolate
broken-hearted
and plain-old down.

aww
itchee-gitchee
gimme-gimme
acca-bacca
shaka-laka
down
down
down by the
riverside

O
"sound of the chain
the gang"
O
bye-bye blackbird-O

but for now
let us close our texts and rest our heads down on our arms.
it's best we take a rest: our lesson for the day is done.
and too
we must call ourselves ready next time we hear the knelling of the old school
                                                                    bell

ready ourselves for the next day's new season in hell

but for now we may well consider ourselves done
having come to the end of the addenda
to the preface for this introduction
of our little history
part one.

GLOSSARY AND NOTES

This collection makes use of phrases, terminology and historically appropriate names of people, places and cultural concepts from a variety of languages deployed in the forging of the New World — French, Spanish, Portuguese, reconstituted (New Orleans) Creole — in addition to American/English of the various periods covered. Variations in spellings and usage (e.g., *expaña*, *yxpañaro*) are intended as examples of how languages collide, fracture, rupture, negotiate, rebuild and reinvent when people, cultures and civilizations come into violent contact.

4 January 1444 Pope Nicholas V grants king of Portugal the right to open trade between Kongo and Portugal. Later that year, African captives are taken from Mauritania to Portugal.

1483 Diogo Cão sails the Atlantic, to the mouth of the River Kongo, returns to Portugal with Kongo "emissaries," who eventually return to Kongo Kingdom in the company of Portuguese soldiers and priests and bearing miscellaneous European goods. See also **Cão, Diogo**, below.

1488 Cape of Good Hope, the southwesternmost point of Africa; first rounded by Bartolomeo Diaz and called by him *Cabo de Tormentas* or "Cape of Storms"; later named *Cabo de Boa Esperança* by João II of Portugal in hope of establishing a direct route from there to India and the Spice Islands.

1516 The Kingdom of Benin formally declares it will "no longer export men, as to continue doing so would strip the kingdom of its power."

African languages referenced in the poem "History":

> **Bambara** primary language of Mali, spoken by about 7 million people;

> **Boulou** also called *Bulu*; language of the Bulu people of Cameroun; spoken by about 1 million people in about a half dozen dialects;

> **Éwondo** language of the Éwondo people of Cameroun; about 600,000 speakers and more than a dozen dialects;

> **Hausa** a Chadic language spoken in Niger and northern Nigeria; also used as a lingua franca throughout West Africa; about 40 million speakers;

Ki-Kongo language of Angola, Democratic Republic of Congo, Congo Republic and throughout Central Africa; a Bantu language with about 7 million speakers;

Kinyarwanda principal language of Rwanda; also spoken in Democratic Republic of Congo, parts of Uganda; Bantu language with 7 million speakers;

Mandara Chadic language spoken in the Mandara Mountains of Cameroun;

Peul also called *Fulani*; West Atlantic language spoken throughout much of West Africa, primarily Senegal, Gambia, Mauritania, Guinea-Bissau, Burkina Faso, Benin, Mali, Niger, Nigeria, Chad, Cameroun; about 16 million speakers;

Sara group of languages spoken in southern Chad; about 300,000 speakers;

Sérère language spoken primarily in the Siné-Saloum region of Senegal and in Gambia;

Shango also called *Sangu*; a Bantu primary language of Central African Republic;

Toupouri Congo language with about 150,000 speakers;

Tshihiba Congo language of the Tshikapa and Bukwanga regions;

Twi an Ashanti language of Ghana;

Wolof primary language of Senegal, also spoken in Gambia and Mauritania; 8-10 million speakers;

Yoruba West African language with more than 20 million speakers in Nigeria, Benin, Togo and Sierra Leone; also spoken in Brazil, Cuba, Colombia and parts of Puerto Rico.

Affonso, King Affonso V (1432–1481), King of Portugal 1438–1477.

aguardiente [Spanish/Portuguese: *agua* + *ardiente*, "burning water"] cane liquor; a coarse, rumlike alcoholic beverage distilled from sugarcane, manufactured and drunk by the slaves of Louisiana, the Caribbean, Latin America; used also as a spiritual offering of libation.

Arawaqi a variant of the name *Arawak*, given to the less warlike Amerindians. In his journals and letters, Columbus praised them for their peaceableness. They were conquered and subdued by the Caribs.

bagasse the fibrous remains of sugarcane once the sugar has been extracted; frequently used in building materials.

canne à sucre [French: *sugarcane*] Creole, *"canne à suc',"* an especially poignant endearment.

Cão, Diogo Portuguese navigator; first European known to have explored the western coast of Africa and the Congo River, in 1482–83 and 1484–86.

castles holding forts or slave castles referenced in the poem "History":

> **Cape Coast** — Ghana; erected in 1653 for the Swedish Africa Company;

> **Cabo de Delgado** — Mozambique; the slave trade continued there until 1877;

> **Elmina** — Ghana; erected in 1482 by the Portuguese;

> **Fort Osu** — Ghana; erected at Accra by the Danes in 1661;

> **Île de Gorée / Goree Island** — home of Senegal's famed *Maison des Esclaves* ("Slave House").The first Slave House was erected in 1536 by the Portuguese; following the French conquest in the 1670s, the newer *Maison des Esclaves* was erected by the French between1780 and 1784;

> **São Tomé** — São Tomé e Principe, island nation in the Gulf of Guinea; erected in 1575 by the Portuguese; now the São Tomé National Museum;

> **São Vicente** — one of the Windward Islands of Cape Verde. Originally settled by the Portuguese in 1456, Cape Verde played a major role in the Atlantic Slave Trade because of its location midway between the western coast of Africa and Europe and the Americas.

Colón, Cristóval or Cristóbal (1451–1506) Italian (*Cristoforo Colombo*) mariner supported in his explorations by the Spanish monarchy; credited with discovery of the Americas (1492) and opening the way for the Atlantic Slave Trade.

Colbert, Jean-Baptiste (1619–1683) author of *Le Code Noir*, the *"Black Codes"* applied throughout the French slave colonies; a key figure in the history of European mercantilism; minister of finance for twenty-two years under King Louis XIV; credited with restoring the French economy by increasing trade, including the French slave trade.

Cooke, Sam (1931–1964) African American soul and gospel singer (The Soul Stirrers); generally cited as the first Soul music superstar and often credited as the Father of Soul Music. His 1960 composition "Chain Gang" was one of many original hits. The version quoted here is from the album, *Sam Cooke Live at the Harlem Square Club 1963* (New York: RCA Victor, 1985).

DOM-TOM [French: acronym for *les Départements d'Outre-mer et les Territoires d'Outre-mer*] French Overseas Departments and Territories include the longtime colonial possessions of: Guadeloupe, Martinique, Guyane, St. Pierre et Miquelon, Mayotte, Réunion, Nouvelle-Calédonie, Wallis and Futuna, and French Polynesia.

Dona Felipe (Perestrello e Moniz), Lady Portuguese noblewoman and wife of Columbus. Historians generally report that she died shortly after the birth of their son Diego, the only legitimate child of Columbus, in 1480 or 1481.

douceur, ma [French: *my sweetness*] Creole endearment.

encomienda [Spanish: *commission, protectorate*] system, beginning in 1493, by which *conquistadores* established Spanish rule and assumed authority over Native peoples of the Americas, including forced labor, taxation and imposition of Catholicism.

Guanahani the original name of Native Americans referred to as "Caribs" and for whom the Caribbean Sea is named. They have traditionally been portrayed as excessively warlike as well as cannibalistic.

Guantanamexe and **Guanaguahana** royal names assigned the elder and younger daughters of the fictional prince of the Caribs, here known only as the *"last of the Guanahani."*

Hayden, Robert (1913–1980); African American poet, perhaps best known for the epic "Middle Passage," "Runagate Runagate" and the sonnet "Frederick Douglass." See his *Collected Poems*, edited by Frederick Glaysher (Liveright, 1985).

Isabel Queen Isabel I; Isabela la Católica de España (1451–1504) queen of Spain; originator (with Ferdinand) of the Inquisition; and patroness of Columbus.

Louis Louis XVI (1754–93) king of France (1774–92) during the French Revolution (1789–91); executed by guillotine January 1793. Execution of his spouse, Marie Antoinette, followed in October of that year.

Marie Galante, Dominica, Juana [now Cuba] and **Española** names given by Columbus to the islands he claimed for the Spanish crown.

Montesquieu Charles-Louis de Secondat, baron de Montesquieu (1689–1755) French author and philosopher; major proponent of Lib¬eralism; best known for 1748 publication of *De l'Esprit des Lois* ("Of the Spirit of the Law"), placed on the Roman Catholic Church's *Index of Forbidden Books* in 1751. Immensely popular, however, the work went through twenty editions during his lifetime. The quoted lines – examples of popular excuses for the need for African slavery – is from the chapter entitled "le Droit de Rendre les Nègres Esclaves" ("The Right to Make Slaves of the Blacks").

Navidad, la [Spanish: *Christmas*] name given by Columbus to the first settlement on Santo Domingo [Haiti] because, he said, it was "born" Christmas 1492.

Nicky Vth, Pope see *4 January 1444*, above.

Qu'on arrive enfin [French: *"So we arrive at last"*]

Rábida, la Dominican convent where Columbus waited while Juan Perez, father confessor to Queen Isabela of Spain, went to Santa Fé to convince the queen to support the navigator's cause.

Répétez s'il-vous-plaît [French: *"Please repeat (after me)"*] phrase traditionally used for teaching by rote in French primary schools.

requerimiento [Spanish: *demand, injunction*] statement of Spanish sovereignty over the Americas, claiming Divine Right under the rule of the Catholic Church, as pronounced in the May 1493 papal bull of Pope Alexander VI.

santa santa fé [Spanish: *holy, holy faith*]; from **Santa Fé**, the military camp of Isabela at Grenada. It was at Santa Fé that Isabela, on the advice of Father Juan Perez, finally received Columbus shortly after reclaiming Grenada from the Moors.

Schoelcher, Victor (1804–1893) author of the Decree of Abolition of 1848 and Caribbean assimilation policy; touted as "savior" of francophone Caribbean and defender of civil rights, the "inheritance of 1789."

slave, slavery Flavius Anicius Julianus Justinianus (483–565), Emperor of Rome (527–565). *Justinian's Code* is a lengthy detailed legal work outlining every aspect of civic and public activity. In parts II-VII, he outlines the legal status of the freeborn, slaves and freedmen. His is the definition of slavery adopted and applied for the Atlantic Slave Trade. The most significant element of the Code applied to modern slavery is the passage *"partus sequitur ventrem,"* which establishes that children follow the condition of the mother: *"Slaves either are born or become so. They are born so when their mother is a slave. . . ."* Justinian's reign is considered by historians to be the apex of the Later Roman Empire.

Tous à la fois [French: *"All together (now)!"*] phrase traditionally used for teaching by rote. See: *Répétez s'il-vous-plaît*, above.

trahison des clercs, la [French, *"the betrayal of the clerks"*] expression traditionally used to refer to the tendency of the mulatto class of the francophone Caribbean to side with the whites.

Yamaye [Arahuacan: *"land of the springs"*] original Arawak name for the island of Jamaica.

Passages quoted in the poem "History":

> **"the fabric of our lives"**: from the Cotton, Incorporated television advertising jingle, *"The touch / the feel of cotton / the fabric of our lives."*

> **"that MAN has indeed become the coin of Africa"**: "I have no hesitation in saying, that three fourths of the slaves sent abroad from Africa are the fruit of native wars, fomented by the avarice and temptation of our own race. I cannot exculpate any commercial nation from this sweeping censure. We stimulate the negro's passions by the introduction of wants and fancies never dreamed of by the simple native, while slavery was an institution of domestic need and comfort alone. But what was once a luxury has now ripened into an absolute necessity; so that MAN, in truth, has become the coin of Africa, and the "legal tender of a brutal trade."

> — "The African Slave Trade," *DeBow's Review: Agricultural, commercial, industrial progress and resources*, March 1855 [vol. 18, no. 3, pp. 297-305].)

In 1846, James D. B. DeBow, a native of Charleston, South Carolina, began publishing his pro-slavery magazine in New Orleans. Originally titled the *Commercial Review of the South and West*, the journal eventually came to be known as *DeBow's Review*. From 1853 to 1857, it was published in Washington, D.C., due to DeBow's appointment there as director of the U.S. Census Bureau. At the start of the Civil War, *DeBow's Review* was the most widely circulated southern periodical.

"ages ago / last night / when we were young": from the Arlen–Harburg composition, "Last Night When We Were Young," as sung by Sarah Vaughan, with Fred Norman's Orchestra (Verve Records, 1959).

"I left my hat / in Haiti!": song and dance routine by Fred Astaire, danced by Astaire, Jane Powell and chorus, in the movie-musical *Royal Wedding* (MGM, 1951); music by Burton Lane, lyrics by Alan Lerner.

"You ain't seen nothing yet": In 1922, Al Jolson (1886–1950) recorded the Bud DeSylva composition "You Ain't Heard Nothing Yet." The line, "You ain't *heard* nothing yet" [emphasis mine], spoken by Jolson, became the first words spoken in a feature film (*The Jazz Singer*, Warner Brothers, 1927), propelled him to instant stardom and became his entr'acte lead-in. Comedic admirers and imitators of Jolson have frequently misquoted the line as "You ain't seen nothing yet!" He is best remembered, however, for his Vaudeville blackface persona. Entertainment legend has it that he adopted blackface because he believed audiences laughed more for black performers than for whites. Jolson is still considered by many to have been the best Vaudeville performer of all time.

ABOUT THE AUTHOR

Brenda Marie Osbey, a New Orleans native, is an author of poetry and prose nonfiction in English and French. Her previous volumes include *All Saints: New and Selected Poems*, which received the 1998 American Book Award. In 2005–2007, she served as the first peer-selected poet laureate of Louisiana.

Studies of her work appear in such critical texts as *Southscapes: Geographies of Race, Region and Literature* by Thadious M. Davis (University of North Carolina Press, 2011); *Forms of Expansion: Recent Long Poems by Women* by Lynn Keller (U. Chicago Press, 1997); *The Future of Southern Letters*, edited by Jefferson Humphries and John Lowe (Oxford, 1996); and such reference works as *Contemporary Authors*; the *Oxford Companion to African American Literature* (1997); the *Dictionary of Literary Biography* (Oxford, 1997); and *Dictionnaire des Créatrices* (Éditions des Femmes, 2011).

Her essays have been published in *The American Voice*, *Georgia Review*, *BrightLeaf*, *Southern Literary Journal* and *Creative Nonfiction*.

She has been a resident fellow of the MacDowell Colony, the Fine Arts Work Center in Provincetown, the Kentucky Foundation for Women, the Virginia Center for the Creative Arts, the Millay Colony, the Camargo Foundation and the Bunting Institute of Radcliffe College, Harvard University. She has received fellowships and awards also from the National Endowment for the Arts, the Louisiana Division of the Arts, and the New Orleans Jazz and Heritage Foundation among others. She is currently Distinguished Visiting Professor of Africana Studies at Brown University.

OTHER POETRY AND SHORT FICTIONS
AVAILABLE FROM TIME BEING BOOKS

YAKOV AZRIEL
Beads for the Messiah's Bride: Poems on Leviticus
In the Shadow of a Burning Bush: Poems on Exodus
Swimming in Moses' Well: Poems on Numbers
Threads from a Coat of Many Colors: Poems on Genesis

EDWARD BOCCIA
No Matter How Good the Light Is: Poems by a Painter

LOUIS DANIEL BRODSKY
At Dock's End: Poems of Lake Nebagamon, Volume Two
At Shore's Border: Poems of Lake Nebagamon, Volume Three
At Water's Edge: Poems of Lake Nebagamon, Volume One
By Leaps and Bounds: Volume Two of *The Seasons of Youth*
The Capital Café: Poems of Redneck, U.S.A.
Catchin' the Drift o' the Draft *(short fictions)*
Combing Florida's Shores: Poems of Two Lifetimes
The Complete Poems of Louis Daniel Brodsky: Volumes One–Four
Dine-Rite: Breakfast Poems
Disappearing in Mississippi Latitudes: Volume Two of *A Mississippi Trilogy*
The Eleventh Lost Tribe: Poems of the Holocaust
Falling from Heaven: Holocaust Poems of a Jew and a Gentile *(Brodsky and Heyen)*
Forever, for Now: Poems for a Later Love
Four and Twenty Blackbirds Soaring
Gestapo Crows: Holocaust Poems
Getting to Unknow the Neighbors *(short fictions)*
A Gleam in the Eye: Volume One of *The Seasons of Youth*
Hopgrassers and Flutterbies: Volume Four of *The Seasons of Youth*
Just Ours: Love Passages with Linda, Volume One
Leaky Tubs *(short fictions)*
Mississippi Vistas: Volume One of *A Mississippi Trilogy*
Mistress Mississippi: Volume Three of *A Mississippi Trilogy*
Nuts to You! *(short fictions)*
Once upon a Small-Town Time: Poems of America's Heartland
Our Time: Love Passages with Linda, Volume Two
Paper-Whites for Lady Jane: Poems of a Midlife Love Affair
Peddler on the Road: Days in the Life of Willy Sypher
Pigskinizations *(short fictions)*
Rabbi Auschwitz: Poems of the Shoah

LOUIS DANIEL BRODSKY *(continued)*

Rated Xmas *(short fictions)*

Saul and Charlotte: Poems Commemorating a Father and Mother

Seizing the Sun and Moon: Volume Three of *The Seasons of Youth*

Shadow War: A Poetic Chronicle of September 11 and Beyond, Volumes One–Five

Showdown with a Cactus: Poems Chronicling the Prickly Struggle Between the Forces of Dubya-ness and Enlightenment, 2003–2006

Still Wandering in the Wilderness: Poems of the Jewish Diaspora

The Swastika Clock: Holocaust Poems

This Here's a Merica *(short fictions)*

The Thorough Earth

Three Early Books of Poems by Louis Daniel Brodsky, 1967–1969: *The Easy Philosopher, "A Hard Coming of It" and Other Poems*, and *The Foul Rag-and-Bone Shop*

Toward the Torah, Soaring: Poems of the Renascence of Faith

A Transcendental Almanac: Poems of Nature

Voice Within the Void: Poems of *Homo supinus*

With One Foot in the Butterfly Farm *(short fictions)*

The World Waiting to Be: Poems About the Creative Process

Yellow Bricks *(short fictions)*

You Can't Go Back, Exactly

HARRY JAMES CARGAS *(editor)*

Telling the Tale: A Tribute to Elie Wiesel on the Occasion of His 65th Birthday — Essays, Reflections, and Poems

JUDITH CHALMER

Out of History's Junk Jar: Poems of a Mixed Inheritance

GERALD EARLY

How the War in the Streets Is Won: Poems on the Quest of Love and Faith

GARY FINCKE

Blood Ties: Working-Class Poems

Reviving the Dead

CHARLES ADÈS FISHMAN

Blood to Remember: American Poets on the Holocaust *(editor)*

Chopin's Piano

In the Path of Lightning: Selected Poems

866-840-4334

HTTP://WWW.TIMEBEING.COM

CB FOLLETT

Hold and Release

One Bird Falling

ALBERT GOLDBARTH

A Lineage of Ragpickers, Songpluckers, Elegiasts & Jewelers: Selected
    Poems of Jewish Family Life, 1973–1995

ROBERT HAMBLIN

Crossroads: Poems of a Mississippi Childhood

From the Ground Up: Poems of One Southerner's Passage to Adulthood

Keeping Score: Sports Poems for Every Season

DAVID HERRLE

Abyssinia, Jill Rush

WILLIAM HEYEN

Erika: Poems of the Holocaust

Falling from Heaven: Holocaust Poems of a Jew and a Gentile *(Brodsky and Heyen)*

The Host: Selected Poems, 1965–1990

Pterodactyl Rose: Poems of Ecology

Ribbons: The Gulf War — A Poem

TED HIRSCHFIELD

German Requiem: Poems of the War and the Atonement of a Third Reich Child

VIRGINIA V. JAMES HLAVSA

Waking October Leaves: Reanimations by a Small-Town Girl

RODGER KAMENETZ

The Missing Jew: New and Selected Poems

Stuck: Poems Midlife

NORBERT KRAPF

Blue-Eyed Grass: Poems of Germany

Looking for God's Country

Somewhere in Southern Indiana: Poems of Midwestern Origins

866-840-4334

HTTP://WWW.TIMEBEING.COM

ADRIAN C. LOUIS
Blood Thirsty Savages

LEO LUKE MARCELLO
Nothing Grows in One Place Forever: Poems of a Sicilian American

GARDNER MCFALL
The Pilot's Daughter
Russian Tortoise

JOSEPH MEREDITH
Hunter's Moon: Poems from Boyhood to Manhood
Inclinations of the Heart

BEN MILDER
From Adolescence to Senescence: A Life in Light Verse
The Good Book Also Says . . . : Numerous Humorous Poems Inspired by
    the New Testament
The Good Book Says . . . : Light Verse to Illuminate the Old Testament
Love Is Funny, Love Is Sad
What's So Funny About the Golden Years
The Zoo You Never Gnu: A Mad Menagerie of Bizarre Beasts and Birds

CHARLES MUÑOZ
Fragments of a Myth: Modern Poems on Ancient Themes

MICHEAL O'SIADHAIL
The Gossamer Wall: Poems in Witness to the Holocaust

CHARLES RAMMELKAMP
Fūsen Bakudan: Poems of Altruism and Tragedy in Wartime

JOSEPH STANTON
A Field Guide to the Wildlife of Suburban O'ahu
Imaginary Museum: Poems on Art

SUSAN TERRIS
Contrariwise